One cannot fully understand the history of Virginia without one of its most important components—religion. Indeed, for more than four centuries, from Jamestown to the present, religion has helped determine the course of history in Virginia and the nation as a whole. If I were asked to develop a list of the key figures in the history of religion in Virginia, John Jasper would be high on it. Without question, he was the most important African-American preacher of the 19th century in Virginia. His sermon, "De Sun Do Move," is considered by many experts to be one of the most influential and widely read messages from the pulpit of its time. I welcome the re-publication of this classic sermon, one that still rings true to the modern ear.

Charles F. Bryan, Jr.
President and CEO
Virginia Historical Society
1988–2008

There is a tradition of simple faith in the history of Baptists. Go far enough back and this tradition is seen to have existed in Baptist churches both among rural white congregations and among African-American congregations wherever they were found. This simple faith might be expressed as: "God saved me through the death and resurrection of His Son; I know who I was and where I was before He saved me; His Spirit is leading me now; and His Word is a reliable and constant guide on the path before me. I can trust His Word fully, for it is Truth from Truth."

John Jasper puts this much more eloquently. "Not ... that I'm the fool to think I knows it all. ... No, friends, I knows my place at the feet of my Master, and there I stays," adding a little later, "It ain't no business of mine whether the sun move or stand still, or whether it stop or go back or rise or set. All that is out of my hands entirely, and I got nothing to say. ... All I ask is that we will take what the Lord say about it and let His will be done about everything. What that will is I can't know except He whisper into my soul or write it in a book. Here's the Book. This is enough for me, and with it to pilot me, I can't get further astray."

At its heart, the sermon, "De Sun Do Move," is a symphony in words of trust, hope, and praise, from a man of simple faith, for others who might come to simple faith, to the one in whom all Truth is to be found. I find in my heart an echo of John Jasper's words, "When you ask me to stop believing in the Lord's Word and to pin my faith to your words, I ain't going to do it. I take my stand by the Bible and rest my case on what it says. I take what the Lord says about my sins, about my Savior, about life, about death, about the world to come, and I take what the Lord say about the sun and moon, and I cares little what the haters of my God chooses to say. Think that I will forsake the Bible? It is my only Book, my hope, the arsenal of my soul's supplies, and I wants nothing else."

I freely admit that there is much of scripture I do not understand. And while I am a scientist, I take my stand where John Jasper takes his: The Bible is true; I can depend on it; and where it may seem that there is a conflict with what science says and what scripture says, the Truth, when all Truth is revealed, will show the Bible to be true. As 1 Corinthians 13:12 puts it, "Now we see things imperfectly as in a cloudy mirror, but then we will see everything with perfect clarity. All that I know now is partial and incomplete, but then I will know everything completely, just as God now knows me completely." (NLT)

Bill Myers
Professor of Chemistry, University of Richmond

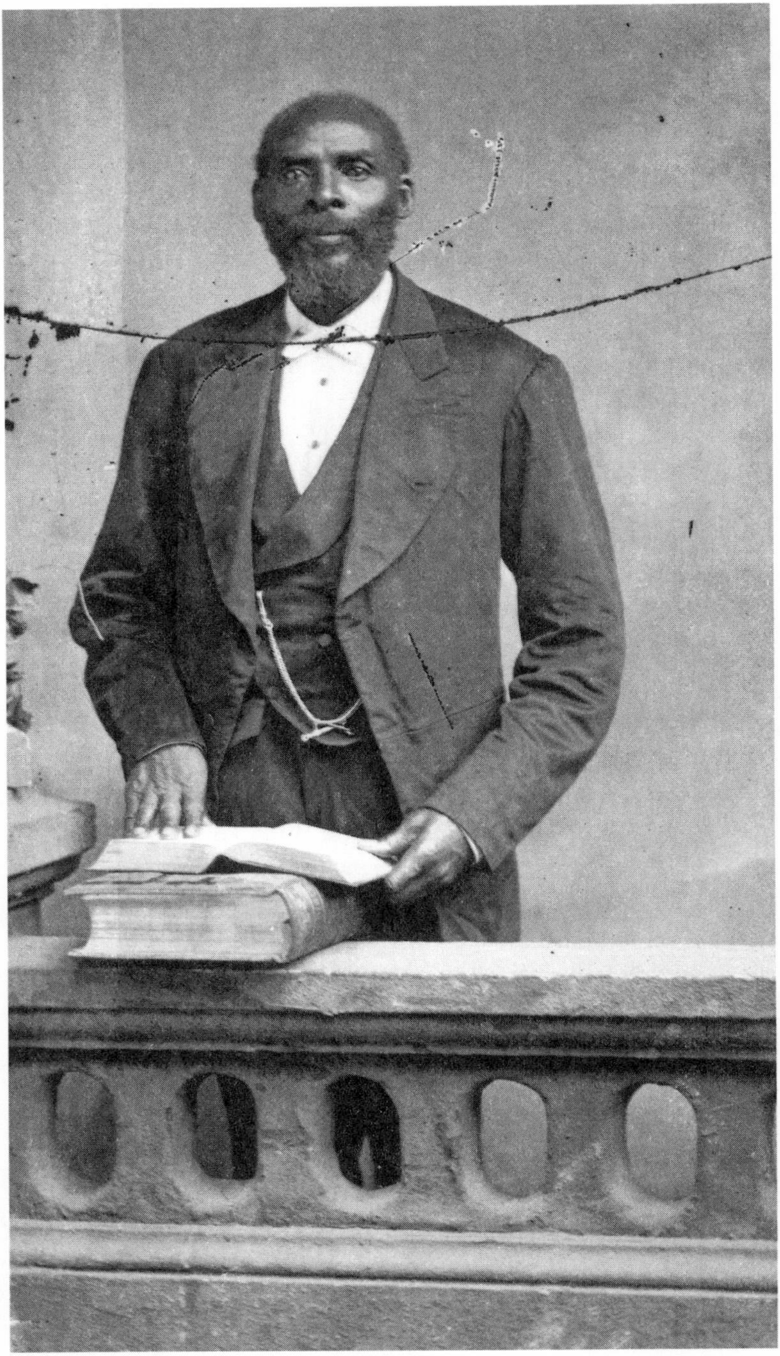

Courtesy of Valentine Richmond History Center

About this Sermon – and this New Translation

They argued that he was ignorant concerning scientific knowledge. But in a smiling, bring-it-on posture, and with a remarkably glorious humility, Reverend John Jasper endeared his audiences as he presented a fundamental truth.

On September 3, 1867 John Jasper organized Richmond's Sixth Mount Zion Baptist Church in a shanty on Brown's Island. (There had been no other Mount Zions in Richmond; Jasper just liked the way "Sixth" sounded.) From that beginning Jasper eventually became one of the most famous and respected preachers in the nation.

Born into slavery on July 4, 1812, John Jasper had become a glorious preacher by 1878 when he first presented his sermon, "De Sun Do Move." Never written by Jasper (he memorized his sermons) and never recorded, this signature sermon resulted in national fame and was presented 273 times at more than 250 venues.

The pastor of Richmond's Grace Street Baptist Church, William Eldridge Hatcher, was a friend and admirer of John Jasper, and in his 1908 biography of Jasper he included "De Sun Do Move" – transcribed from his personal audience and from newspaper accounts. Although Hatcher noted that Jasper spoke with "almost unspellable"

Reverend John Jasper, 1870s; photographer: probably D.H. Anderson; Cook Collection, Valentine Richmond History Center.

dialect, Hatcher nevertheless took a stab at spelling the dialect in his published transcription of the sermon. The result was – for 100 years now – our best printed record of this famous sermon. The result was also painstakingly difficult to read.

The new translation in this booklet – based on a careful word-by-word and line-by-line attention to Hatcher's transcription – simply presents a readable version that is accessible to today's audiences. The sermon is important, and it should be read. This new translation is – as Tyrone Nelson, pastor of today's Sixth Mount Zion Baptist Church, says – "bringing the words of our founder back to life."

—*John Bryan, 2008, Richmond*

"I crep 'long mighty tejus,

gittin' a crum here an dar

untel I cud read de Bible

by skippin' de long words,

tolerable well. Dat was da

start uv my eddicashun"

—from the William E. Hatcher transcription

"DE SUN DO MOVE."

Reverend John Jasper

newly translated by John Bryan

*The famous signature sermon of a former slave
and founder of Richmond's historic Sixth Mount Zion
Baptist Church.*

Charles Creek Publishing

"De Sun Do Move"
Reverend John Jasper
newly translated by John Bryan

Charles Creek Publishing
P.O. Box 25071
Richmond, VA 23260-5071
charlescreekpub@aol.com

Library of Congress Control Number: 2008932999

Publisher's Cataloging-in-Publication
(Provided by Quality Books, Inc.)

Jasper, John, 1812-1901.
    "De sun do move" : the famous signature sermon of a former slave and founder of Richmond's historic Sixth Mount Zion Baptist Church / John Jasper ; newly translated by John Bryan. — 1st ed.
      p. cm.
      ISBN-13: 978-0-9818194-5-7
      ISBN-10: 0-9818194-5-1

    1. Sermons, American—African American authors.
2. Sermons, American—19th century. 3. Baptists—Sermons.
4. Religion and science—Sermons. 5. Virginia—History
—19th century. I. Bryan, John, 1949– II. Title.

BX6452.J37 2008   252'.061
                 QBI08-600217

First Edition

Design by Ben Cornatzer; illustration of Rev. Jasper courtesy of Sixth Mount Zion Baptist Church; clouds from www.GettyImages.com.

Printed in the United States of America

CONTENTS

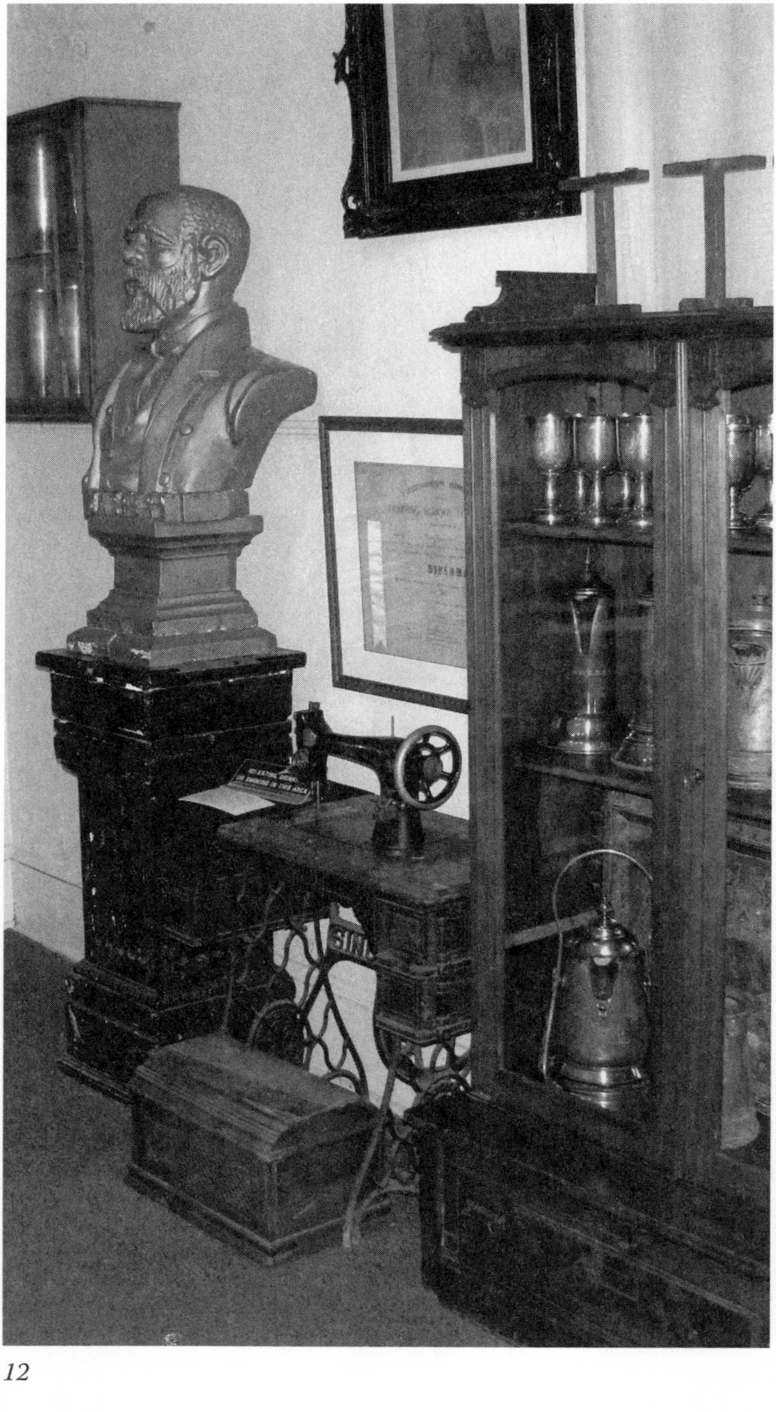
Courtesy of Sixth Mount Zion Baptist Church

Acknowledgements

Thanks first to Benjamin Ross, Church Historian at Sixth Mount Zion Baptist Church, who welcomed me for my first visit to the church, showed me the John Jasper archives and museum, and embraced this project. Every Richmonder and visitor should experience John Jasper and Sixth Mount Zion Baptist Church through the guidance of Benjamin Ross.

I am grateful for my very first introduction to this sermon via the early 1980s gift shop of the Valentine Richmond History Center in which I purchased the sermon in the form of a publication of the Dietz Press. Now long out of print, I purchased and gifted many copies of that Dietz publication through the years.

Appreciation goes to Jim Ukrop and Walter Witschey for their willingness to write the Foreword and Introduction for this publication. Thanks also to my cousins – historian Charlie Bryan and scientist Bill Myers – for their good words about the importance of this publication.

I am grateful for my year on the staff, and now as a volunteer, of Baptist Theological Seminary at Richmond – a great institution with intellectually stimulating colleagues. The BTSR atmosphere was a conducive and invigorating backdrop for my work on this project. The

The John Jasper Archives and Museum at Sixth Mount Zion Baptist Church.

reader will note that proceeds from this publication
are donated to BTSR and to Sixth Mount Zion
Baptist Church.

I thank designer Ben Cornatzer for making me realize
that this sermon is worthy of much more than the design-
print-and-staple request that I first presented to him.

And finally and ultimately I thank and acknowledge
Tyrone Nelson for his willingness to help this stranger
in this production of a brand new version of his church's
most important sermon ever. And I thank those whom
Reverend Nelson represents as pastor and servant-leader:
Sixth Mount Zion's congregation members who enhanced
my enjoyment of the church's Sunday worship service.

—*John Bryan*

Foreword *by Jim Ukrop*

How magnificent it is that the words so zealously proclaimed by Reverend John Jasper in his sermon "De Sun Do Move" have been preserved for us. I applaud the Baptist Theological Seminary at Richmond for making them available. For in this sermon, we clearly are drawn into the passion that Reverend Jasper had for his Lord and for delivering that faith to his audience some 130 years ago. In a time of enlightenment with industry and scientific discovery capturing the inquisitiveness and imagination of man, Reverend Jasper was reminding the sheep of his pasture that the source of all was our almighty God.

The words of an old hymn, penned by Frederick W. Faber in 1863, whose own life span was bracketed by two wars, ring in our ears as we read his defense of God's word in the midst of scientific debate.

> *"Faith of our fathers, living still,*
> *In spite of dungeon, fire and sword;*
> *Oh, how our hearts beat high with joy*
> *When'er we hear that glorious word!*
> *Faith of our fathers, holy faith!*
> *We will be true to thee till death."*
> ("Faith of Our Fathers"; Frederick W. Faber, 1849)

Christians from every land, from every race, give thanks for those people of great faith who lived that faith in extraordinary ways, unwavering in any circumstance to lead us along our path. They may have been our parents or grandparents, aunts or uncles, friends or acquaintances, ministers or teachers. Whether only one or many, we are blessed by their pledge of faith and commitment to pass it on.

Reverend Jasper, the noted pastor of Richmond's Sixth Mount Zion Baptist Church in an age gone by, was just such a light to his world. Read for yourself the words of this text and you will understand why Reverend Jasper was invited to deliver this sermon to so many, so often, in so many prominent venues. Whether our personal perspective is more liberal, moderate, or fundamental, we all are strengthened when we have access to passionate faith such as found here in "De Sun Do Move."

I highly encourage you to read this sermon and let Reverend John Jasper's passion for his Lord and the Word of God speak to you in the way it will. I remain grateful to the Baptist Theological Seminary at Richmond for making it available to us all.

James E. Ukrop is Chairman of the Boards of Ukrop's Super Markets and First Market Bank, both headquartered in Richmond, Virginia. He has served on several corporate boards and is active in leadership roles at The College of William and Mary and in the Richmond non-profit community.

Introduction *by Walter Witschey*

John Jasper's charismatic appeal is as compelling today as on those hot sun-drenched days 130 years ago when he first delivered "De Sun Do Move."

We are tempted to label as "quaint," Jasper's sparring with the science of his day. Why indeed not build a railroad to the sun if we know how far away it is?

The power of Jasper's words, however, is in his fundamental grasp of eternal truths. The power of the Lord is omnipotent. The Lord God of Hosts hears when his people call out to him. "The Word of the Lord endureth forever."

Jasper's sermon, and its often contentious Socratic debate between science and religion, also has a modern immediacy in today's culture wars. Since Darwin's time, about fifteen years before the sermon was first delivered, people who read the Word literally have been challenged to integrate modern science into their faith and do so with difficulty.

The result in 2008 is a rip in our social fabric, a pitched battle led by those who wish to promulgate their own religion in the science classes of the public schools. Such efforts are labeled creationism or intelligent design. They carry pseudo-scientific trappings under headings such as "irreducible complexity." They attempt to propagandize and diminish our faith, as well as inculcate students with misunderstandings about the nature of science and its inquiries about the observable world.

Most mainstream Christians today integrate their faith with modern science and its technological outpourings. They may hold a less-than-full comprehension of modern cosmology, but they also hold an abiding faith that the Lord continues to reveal himself and His Creation to humans—and that modern science is one aspect of the revelation.

The revelations concern more than just the distance to the sun, about which Jasper was well-informed. Jasper said,

> *You set yourself up to tell me how far it is from here to the sun. You think you got it down to a nice point. You say it is 3,339,002 miles from the earth to the sun. That's what you say. Another one say that the distance is 12,000,000; another got it to 27,000,000. I hears that the great Isaak Newton worked it up to 28,000,000 and later on the philosophers give another raise to 50,000,000. The last one gits it bigger than all the others, up to 90,000,000.*

Today we use 93 million miles as our best estimate for an average of the constantly changing distance between ourselves and our sun. But we know more...

The great NASA observatories provide a flood of new insights about the Creation, its past and its future. Modern estimates for the ancient age of the earth (4.6 billion years) and the age of the universe we see (13.7 billion years), leave us more in awe of the Creation, not less.

Isaac Watts paraphrased Psalm 90 this way:

A thousand ages in Thy sight,
　Are like an evening gone;
Short as the watch that ends the night,
　Before the rising sun.

We now see Creation through the eyes of the Hubble Space Telescope as breathtaking and ancient beyond our understanding, and in a powerfully inspiring sense.

After 130 years, Jasper's sermon rings in our ears—it captures the passion of a man speaking with unique eloquence about his own faith journey, and it compels us to join with him on the grand journey of faith.

Dr. Walter R. T. Witschey is Professor of Anthropology and Science Education at Longwood University, where he teaches archaeology and geographic information systems. From 1992-2007 he was the Director (CEO) of the Science Museum of Virginia. He is past president of the Virginia Academy of Science. He was raised in the Baptist tradition in Charleston, West Virginia, and today is a Presbyterian Elder.

SA 43

SIXTH MOUNT ZION
BAPTIST CHURCH

The Rev. John Jasper, born a slave in Fluvanna
County on 4 July 1812, organized the Sixth
Mount Zion Baptist Church congregation in
Richmond on 3 Sept. 1867 in a former Confed-
erate stable on Brown's Island. A nationally cel-
ebrated preacher, Jasper was best known for
his 1878 sermon De Sun Do Move, which he
later delivered by invitation more than 250 times.
He died on 30 Mar. 1901 and is buried in
Woodlawn Cemetery in Richmond. In 1869, the
congregation moved to this site. The present
church (built 1887-1890) was remodeled in 1925
in the Gothic Revival style by the noted
black architect Charles T. Russell.

A Letter to the Reader *by Tyrone Nelson*

The heart of a great leader is examined as we read the words of this timeless sermon penned by our founder, the Reverend John Jasper. For decades now, the Sixth Mount Zion Baptist Church, located in the capital city of Richmond, Virginia, has become a tourist attraction and haven for those on a quest to see deeper into the soul of this prophet. Reenactments of Reverend Jasper's moving testimonies and sermons have captivated thousands, all marveling at how his moving and passionate words caused grown men to cry and women to faint.

As a slave committed to both education and faith, Jasper's vigor and wisdom enabled many to explore the possibilities of wonder that stretch far beyond our human understanding. For many who approach life from a religious context, the line between spirituality and science is rarely crossed. Primarily, one views life through the lens of either science or religion. However, Reverend Jasper more than a century ago wrestled with the phenomenon of exploring life through the eye of faith and reason. Jasper's effortless leadership catapulted this community of faith into national prominence as one of the fastest growing and stable African American churches in the 19th and early 20th centuries. This inquiry into the unknown and dependence upon his knowledge of the Bible gives us courage to do the same in the 21st century.

For over 140 years, the church that Jasper founded has served the Jackson Ward and Greater Richmond Metropolitan area. Still, the spirit of John Jasper continues to permeate the walls of the church located at the corner of St. John and Duval Street. The faith of our founder rings true even now. With every prayer prayed, song sung, and sermon preached, the faith of our founder rings true. As the church feeds the hungry, provides shelter for the homeless, advocates for the disenfranchised, and financially supports the efforts of organizations that work to meet the needs of others, the faith of our founder rings true. Whenever the doors of our church are open, when families come together with men and women providing unhindered leadership, people are empowered, and the holistic development of community is the focus, the faith of our founder rings true.

It is my earnest hope that the words of this sermon renew your commitment to the faith that has encouraged and motivated so many to continue this lifelong journey toward righteousness. The Sixth Mount Zion Baptist Church commends and thanks the Baptist Theological Seminary for the time and effort put into bringing the words of our founder back to life. Live on John Jasper! "De Sun Do Move, yes, The Son Does Move!"

Native Richmonder Reverend Tyrone E. Nelson, pastor of Sixth Mount Zion Baptist Church, holds degrees of Associate of Science in Business Administration from J. Sergeant Reynolds Community College, Bachelor of Science in Business Administration from Virginia Commonwealth

*University, and Master of Divinity from Virginia Union
University's Samuel DeWitt Proctor School of Theology.
Reverend Nelson serves on a variety of community, church
and civic boards and committees in Richmond and beyond. Since Nelson's arrival as Pastor in 2005, Sixth
Mount Zion Baptist Church has experienced growth in its
membership and ministries, and is currently home to the
Center for Christian Education and Spiritual Development and its Saturday Night Live Worship services. It
has become a diverse church that meets the needs of its
children, youth, adults, and seniors.*

*Sixth Mount Zion Baptist Church, 14 West Duval Street,
Richmond, VA 23220*

www.smzbc.org

"DE SUN DO MOVE."

Reverend John Jasper

"Gord cunverted my soul,

an' I reckin 'bout de fust

an' main thing dat I begged

de Lord ter give me wuz

de power ter und'stan'

His Word."

"DE SUN DO MOVE."

Reverend John Jasper

Allow me to say that when I was a young man and a slave I knowed nuthin' worth talkin' about concerning books. They was sealed mysteries to me, but I tell you I longed to break the seal. I thirsted for the bread of learnin'. When I seen books, I ached to get into them, for I knowed that they had the stuff for me, and I wanted to taste their contents. But most of the time they was barred against me.

By the mercy of the Lord a thing happened. I got a room-fellow – he was a slave too – and he had learned to read. In the dead of the night he give me lessons out of the New York Spellin' Book. It was hard pullin', I tell you – harder on him for he knowed just a little and it made him sweat to try to beat somethin' into my hard head. It was worse with me. Up the hill every step, but when I got the light of the lesson into my noodle I fairly shouted. But I knowed I was not a scholar.

The consequence was I crept along mighty tedious, getting a crumb here and there until I could read the Bible – by skippin' the long words – tolerable well. That was the start of my education – that is, what little I got.

I make mention of that young man. The years have fled away since then, but I ain't forgot my teacher and never shall. I thank my Lord for him, and I carries his memory in my heart.

About seven months after my getting' to readin', God converted my soul and I reckon about the first and main thing that I begged the Lord to give me was the power to understand His Word. I ain't braggin', and I hates self-praise, but I'm bound to speak the thankful word. I believes in my heart that my prayer to understand the Scripture was heard. Since that time I ain't cared about nothin' 'cept to study and preach the Word of God.

Not, my brethren, that I'm the fool to think I knows it all. Oh, my Father, no! Far from it. I don't hardly understand myself, nor half of the things around me, and there is millions of things in the Bible too deep for Jasper, and some of them too deep for everybody. I don't carry the keys to the Lord's closet, and He ain't told me to peep in, and if I did I'm so stupid I wouldn't know it when I see it. No, friends, I knows my place at the feet of my Master, and there I stays.

But I can read the Bible and get the things what lay on top of the soil. Other than the Bible I know nothin' extra about the sun. I see his course as he rides up there so grand and mighty in the sky, but there is heaps about that flaming orb that is too much for me. I know that the sun shines powerfully and puts down its light in floods, and yet that is nothin' compared with the light that flashes in my mind from the pages of God's book. But you knows all that. I knows that the sun burns – oh how it did burn in them July days. I tell you he cooked the skin on my back many a day when I was hoein' in the corn field. But you knows all that, and yet that is nothin' to the divine fire that burns in the souls of God's children. Can't you feel it, brethren?

But about the course of the sun, I have got that. I have done ranged through the whole blessed Book and wrote down every last thing the Bible has to say about the movements of the sun. I got all that pat and safe. And let me say that if I don't give it to you straight, if I gets one word crooked or wrong, you just holler out "Hold on there, Jasper, you ain't got that straight," and I'll beg your pardon. If I don't tell the truth, then you march up on these steps here and tell me I's a liar, and I'll take it. I fears I do lie sometimes – I'm so sinful, I find it hard to do right. But my God don't lie and he ain't put no lie in the book of eternal truth, and if I give you what the Bible say, then I'm bound to tell the truth.

I got to take you all this afternoon on an excursion to a great battlefield. Most folks like to see fights – some is mighty fond of getting into fights, and some is mighty quick to run down the back alley when there is a battle goin' on. This time I'll escort you to a scene where you shall witness a curious battle. It took place soon after Israel got in the Promised Land.

You remember, the people of Gideon made friends with God's people when they first entered Canaan and they was smart to do it. But, just the same, it got them into an awful fuss. The cities round about there flared up at that, and they all joined their forces and said they were going to mop the Gideon people off of the ground, and they bunched all their armies together and went up to do it. When they come up so bold and brave the Gideonites was scared out of their senses, and they sent word to Joshua that they was in trouble and he must run up there and get them out. Joshua had the heart of a lion and he was up there directly.

They had an awful fight, sharp and bitter, but you might know that General Joshua was not up there to get whipped. He prayed and he fought and the hours got away too fast for him, and so he asked the Lord to issue a special order that the sun hold up awhile and that the moon furnish plenty of moonshine down on the lowest part of the fighting grounds. As a fact, Joshua was so drunk with the battle, so thirsty for the blood of the enemies of the Lord, and so wild with the victory that he told the sun to stand still until he could finish his job.

What did the sun do? Did he glare down in firey wrath and say, "What you talking about my stopping for, Joshua; I ain't never started yet. Been here all the time, and it would smash up everything if I was to start"? No, he ain't say that. But what did the Bible say? That's what I asked to know. It say that it was at the voice of Joshua that it stopped.

I don't say it stopped; it ain't for Jasper to say that, but the Bible, the Book of God, say so. But I say this: nothin' can stop until it has first started. So I knows what I'm talking about. The sun was travelin' along there through the sky when the order come. He hitched his red ponies and made quite a call on the land of Gideon. He perched up there in the skies just as friendly as a neighbor what comes to borrow something, and he stand up there and he look like he enjoyed the way Joshua waxes them wicked armies. And the moon, she wait down in the low ground there, and pours out her light and look just as calm and happy as if she was waitin' for her escort. They never budged, neither of them, long as the Lord's army needed a light to carry on the battle.

I don't read when it was that Joshua hitched up and drove on, but I suppose it was when the Lord told him to go. Anybody knows that the sun didn't stay there all the time. It stopped for business, and went on when it got through. This is about all that I has to do with this particular

"I know dat de sun shines powerfly an' po's down its light in floods, an' yet dat is nuthin' compared wid de light dat flashes in my min' frum de pages of Gord's book."

case. I done showed you that this part of the Lord's word teaches you that the sun stopped, which shows that he was movin' before that, and that he went on afterwards. I told you that I would prove this and I've done it, and I defies anybody to say that my point ain't made.

I told you in the first part of this discourse that the Lord God is a man of war. I expect by now you begin to see it is so. Don't you admit it? When the Lord come to see Joshua in the day of his fears and warfare and actually made the sun stop stone-still in the heavens, so the fight can rage on until all the foes is slain, you're obliged to understand that the God of peace is also the man of war. He can use both peace and war to help the righteous, and to scatter the host of the aliens.

A man talked to me last week about the laws of nature, and he say they can't possibly be upset, and I had to laugh right in his face. As if the laws of anything was greater than my God who is the lawgiver for everything. My Lord is great. He rules in the heavens, in the earth, and down under the ground. He is great, and greatly to be praised. Let all the people bow down and worship before Him.

But let us get along, for there is quite a big lot more coming on. Let us take next the case of Hezekiah. He was one of them kings of Judah – a mighty sorry lot I must say them kings was, for the most part. I inclines to think Hezekiah was about the highest in the general average, and he was no mighty man hisself.

Well, Hezekiah he got sick. I dare say that a king when he gits his crown and finery off, and when he is prostrate with mortal sickness, he gits about as common lookin' and grunts and rolls, and is about as scary as the rest of us poor mortals. We know that Hezekiah was in a low state of mind, full of fears, and in a terrible trouble. The fact is, the Lord stripped him of all his glory and landed him in the dust. He told him that his hour had come, and that he had better square up his affairs, for death was at the door.

Then it was that the king fell low before God; he turned his face to the wall; he cried, he moaned, he begged the Lord not to take him out of the world yet. Oh how good is our God. The cry of the king moved His heart, and, He tell him He goin' to give him another show. Ain't only the kings that the Lord hears; the cry of the prisoner, the wail of the bondsman, the tears of the dying robber, the prayers of the backslider, the sobs of the woman that was a sinner, might apt to touch the heart of the Lord. It look like it's hard for the sinner to get so far off or so far down in the pit that his cry can't reach the ear of the merciful Savior.

But the Lord do even better than this for Hezekiah. He tell him He going to give him a sign by which he'd know that what He said was coming to pass. I ain't acquainted with them sun dials that the Lord told Hezekiah about, but anybody that has got a grain of sense knows that they was the clocks of them old times and they marked the travels of the sun by them dials. When, therefore, God told the king that He would make the shadow go back-ward, it must have been just like putting the hands of the clock back, but, mark you, Isaiah expressly say that the sun returned ten degrees.

There you are! Ain't that the movement of the sun? Bless my soul. Hezekiah's case beat Joshua's. Joshua stopped the sun, but here the Lord make the sun walk back ten degrees; and yet they say that the sun stand stone-still and never move a peg. It look to me he move round

"It ain't no bizniss uv mine wedder

de sun move or stan still, or wedder it

stop or go back or rise or set.

All dat is out er my han's 'tirely,

an' I got nuthin' ter say.

I got no the-o-ry on de subjik.

All I ax is dat we will take

wat de Lord say"

might brisk and is ready to go any way that the Lord orders him to go.

I wonder if any of them philosophers is 'round here this afternoon. I'd like to take a square look at one of them and ask him to explain this matter. He can't do it, my brethren. He knows a heap about books, maps, figures and long distances, but I defy him to take up Hezekiah's case and explain it off. He can't do it. The Word of the Lord is my defense and bulwark, and I fears not what men can say or do; my God gives me the victory.

Allow me, my friends, to put myself square about this movement of the sun. It ain't no business of mine whether the sun move or stand still, or whether it stop or go back or rise or set. All that is out of my hands entirely, and I got nothing to say. I got no theory on the subject. All I ask is that we will take what the Lord say about it and let His will be done about everything. What that will is I can't know except He whisper into my soul or write it in a book. Here's the Book. This is enough for me, and with it to pilot me, I can't get further astray.

But I ain't done with you yet. As the song says, there's more to follow.

I invite you to hear the first verse in the seventh chapter of the book of Revelation. What do John, under the power of the Spirit, say? He say he saw four angels standing on the four corners of the earth, holding the four winds of the earth, and so forth. Allow me to ask if the earth is round, where do it keep its corners? A flat square thing has corners, but tell me where is the corner of an apple or a marble or a cannon ball or a silver dollar?

If there is any one of them philosophers what's been taking so many cracks at my old head about here, he is cordially invited to step forward and square up this vexing business. I'm here to tell you that you can't square a circle, but it looks like these great scholars done learn how to circle the square. If they can do it, let them step to the front and do the trick.

But, my brethren, in my poor judgment, they can't do it; tain't in them to do it. They is on the wrong side of the Bible; they's on the outside of the Bible, and there's where the trouble comes in with them. They done got out of the breastworks of the truth, and as long as they stay there the light of the Lord will not shine on their path. I ain't caring so much about the sun - though it's mighty convenient to have it - but my trust is in the Word of the Lord. Long as my feet is flat on the solid rock, no man can move me. I'm getting' my orders from the God of my salvation.

The other day a man with a high collar and side whiskers come to my house. He was one nice Northern gentleman what think a heap of us colored people in the south. They are lovely folks and I honors them very much. He seem from the start kind of strict and cross with me, and after a while he broke out furious and fretted, and he say: "Allow me Mister Jasper to give you some plain advice. This nonsense about the sun moving is disgracing your race all over the country, and as a friend of your people, I come to say it's got to stop."

Ha! Ha! Ha! Mr. Sam Hargrove never hardly smash me that way. It was equal to one of them old overseers way back yonder. I tell him that if he'll show me I's wrong, I'll give it all up.

My! My! Ha! Ha! He sail in on me in such a storm about science, new discoveries, and the Lord only knows what all, I never heard before, and then he tell me my race is urging me, and poor old Jasper must shut up his fool mouth.

When he got through – it look like he never would – I tell him John Jasper ain't set up to be no scholar, and don't know the philosophies, and ain't trying to hurt his people, but is working day and night to lift them up, and his foot is on the rock of eternal truth. There he stand and there he is going to stand until Gabriel sounds the judgment note.

So I say to the gentleman what scolded me up so that I hear him make his remarks - but I ain't heard what he got his Scripture from - and that between him and the Word of the Lord I take my stand by the Word of God every time. Jasper ain't mad: he ain't fighting nobody; he ain't been appointed janitor to run the sun: he ain't nothing but the servant of God and a lover of the Everlasting Word.

What do I care about the sun? The day comes on when the sun will be called from his racetrack, and his light squinched out forever; the moon shall turn to blood, and this earth be consumed with fire. Let them go; that won't scare me nor trouble God's elected people, for the Word of the Lord shall endure forever, and on that Solid Rock we stand and shall not be moved.

Is I got you satisfied yet? Has I proven my point? Oh, ye whose hearts is full of unbelief! Is you still holding out? I reckon the reason you say the sun don't move is because you are so hard to move yourself. You is a real trial to me, but never mind; I ain't giving you up yet, and never will. Truth is mighty; it can break the heart of stone, and I must fire another arrow of truth out of the quiver of the Lord.

If you has a copy of God's Word about your person, please turn to that minor profit, Malachi, what write the last book in the old Bible, and look at chapter the first, verse eleven; what do it say? I better read it, for I got a notion you critics don't carry any Bible in your pockets every day in the week.

Here is what it says: "Far from the rising of the sun even under the going down of the same My name shall be great among the Gentiles . . . My name shall be great among the heathen, says the Lord of hosts." How do that suit you? It look like that ought to fix it. This time it's the Lord of hosts Hisself that is doing the talking, and He is talking on a wonderful and glorious subject. He is telling of the spreading of His Gospel, of the coming of His last victory over the Gentiles, and the worldwide glories that at the last He is to get.

Oh, my brethren, what a time that will be. My soul takes wing as I anticipate with joy that millennium day! The glories as they shine before my eyes blinds me, and I forgets the sun and moon and stars. I just remembers that along about those last days that the sun and moon will go out of business, for they won't be needed no more. Then will King Jesus come back to see His people, and He will be sufficient light of the world. Joshua's battles will be over. Hezekiah won't need no sun dial, and the sun and moon will fade out before the glorious splendors of the New Jerusalem.

But what the matter with Jasper? I almost forgot my business, and almost going to shouting over the far away glories of the second coming of my Lord. I beg pardon, and will try to get back to my subject. I have to do as the sun in Hezekiah's case – fall back a few degrees.

"John Jasper ain' set up to be

no scholur, an' doant kno de

ferlosophiz, an' ain' tryin' ter hurt

his peopul, but is wurkin' day an'

night ter lif 'em up, but his foot is

on de rock uv eternal truff."

In that part of the Word that I give you from Malachi – that the Lord Hisself spoke – He declares that His glory is going to spread. Spread? Where? From the rising of the sun to the going down of the same. What? Don't say that, does it? That's exactly what it says. Ain't that clear enough for you?

The Lord pity these doubting Thomases. Here is enough to settle it all and cure the worst cases. Walk up here, wise folks, and get your medicine. Where is them high collared philosophers now? What they skulking round in the brush for? Why don't you get out in the broad afternoon light, and fight for your colors?

Ah, I understands it; you got no answer. The Bible is against you, and in your conscience you are convicted.

But I hears you back there. What you whispering about? I know; you say you sent me some papers and I never answer them. Ha, ha, ha! I got them. The difficulty 'bout them papers you sent me is that they did not answer me. They never mention the Bible one time.

You think so much of yourself and so little of the Lord God and thinks what you say is so smart that you can't even speak of the Word of the Lord. When you ask me to stop believing in the Lord's Word and to pin my faith to your words, I ain't going to do it. I take my stand by the Bible and rest my case on what it says. I take what the Lord says about my sins, about my Savior, about life, about death, about the world to come, and I take what the Lord say about the sun and moon, and I cares little what the haters of my God chooses to say. Think that I will forsake the Bible? It is my only Book, my hope, the arsenal of my soul's supplies, and I wants nothing else.

But I got another word for you yet. I done work over them papers that you sent me without date and without your name. You deals in figures and thinks you are bigger than the Archangels. Let me see what you done say.

You set yourself up to tell me how far it is from here to the sun. You think you got it down to a nice point. You say it is 3,339,002 miles from the earth to the sun. That's what you say. Another one say that the distance is 12,000,000; another got it to 27,000,000. I hears that the great Isaak Newton worked it up to 28,000,000 and later on the philosophers give another raise to 50,000,000. The last one gits it bigger than all the others, up to 90,000,000.

Don't any of them agree exactly and so they runs a guess game, and the last guess is always the biggest. Now, when these guessers can have a convention in Richmond and all agree upon the same thing, I'd be glad to hear from you again, and I does hope that by that time you won't be ashamed of your name.

Heaps of railroads has been built since I saw the first one when I was fifteen years old, but I ain't hear tell of a railroad built yet to the sun. I don't see why if they can measure the distance to the sun, they might not get up a railroad or a telegraph and enable us to find something else about it than merely how far off the sun is. They tell me that a cannon ball could make the trip to the sun in twelve years. Why don't they send it? It might be rigged up with quarters for a few philosophers on the inside and fixed up for a comfortable ride. They would need twelve years' rations and a heap of changes of mighty thick clothes when they start and mighty thin ones when they get there.

"Dey tell me dat a kannun ball cu'd

mek de trip ter de sun in twelve

years. Why doan' dey send it? It

might be rig'd up wid quarturs fur a

few furloserfurs on de inside an' fixed

up fur er kumfurterble ride."

Oh, my brethren, these things make you laugh, and I don't blame you for laughing, except it's always sad to laugh at the follies of fools. If we could laugh at them about their countings, we might well laugh day and night. What cuts into my soul is, that all these men seem to me that they is hitting at the Bible. That's what stirs my soul and fills me with righteous wrath. Little cares I what they says about the sun, provided they let the Word of the Lord alone.

But never mind. Let the heathen rage and the people imagine a vain thing. Our King shall break them in pieces and dash them down. But blessed be the name of our God, the Word of the Lord endureth forever. Stars may fall, moons may turn to blood, and the sun set to rise no more, but Thy Kingdom, oh Lord, is from everlasting to everlasting.

But I has a word this afternoon for my own brethren. They is the people for whose souls I got to watch – for them I got to stand and report at the last – they is my sheep and I's the shepherd, and my soul is knit to them forever.

Tain't for me to be troubling you with these questions about them heavenly bodies. Our eyes goes far beyond the smaller stars; our home is clean out of sight of them twinkling orbs; the chariot that will come to take us to our Father's mansion will roll out by them flickering lights and never halt 'til it brings us in clear view of the throne of the Lamb.

Don't hitch your hopes to no sun nor stars; your home is got Jesus for its light, and your hopes must travel up that way.

I preach this sermon just for to settle the minds of my few brethren, and repeats it cause friends wish to hear it, and

I hopes it will do honor to the Lord's Word. But nothing short of the pearly gates can satisfy me, and I charge, my people, fix your feet on the solid Rock, your hearts on Calvary, and your eyes on the throne of the Lamb. These strifes and griefs will soon get over; we shall see the King in His glory and be at ease. Go on, go on, ye ransom of the Lord; shout His praises as you go, and I shall meet you in the city of the New Jerusalem, where we shan't need the light of the sun, for the Lamb of the Lord is the light of the saints.

IN MEMORY OF
REV. JOHN JASPER, D. D.
1812 — 1901.

Afterword *by John Bryan*

It is a chilly, drizzly, first Sunday morning in April 2008. I am greeted by deep rhythms of electric guitar, full pews of worshipers – some standing and clapping – bright little girls with pigtails swinging, and a dark brown outstretched hand. I am a lone, unannounced, and un-planned stranger here. I know nobody in this historic church – Reverend John Jasper's legacy. Many white visitors would have been here 125 years ago – here to experience Jasper's tall, passionate, persuasive, eloquence – but today I am the only one.

My visit is compelled by my interest in Jasper's most famous sermon – "De Sun Do Move" – and my desire to experience his church and to witness the current pastor, Reverend Tyrone Nelson.

The context of this day is notable. Just a few days ago Reverend Jeremiah Wright – Senator Barack Obama's longtime pastor – was introduced to national audiences via video clips of him proclaiming anti-government, anti-white, anti-lots-of-stuff hate speech. At least that was the media's spin. Some "experts" are saying this is normal in "the black church." And in response to that notion is the heated retort that there is no such entity as "the black church." That's as preposterous as assigning a homogeny to "the white church."

Detail of window in Sixth Mount Zion Baptist Church honoring Rev. Jasper.

Today's context also includes the freshness of my participation in the recent New Baptist Covenant meeting in Atlanta attended by 15,000+ Baptists — half white, half black. This was the first time in 150 years that so many species of white and black Baptists had convened. Although deeply divided on deep-seated social and theological issues, there were three days of harmony as we all abided by the one ground rule: do not criticize any other person or any other group.

And a third part of today's context is a metaphor: a photograph and article in this morning's *Richmond Times-Dispatch* newspaper featuring fish being released into Byrd Park's Shields Lake. This is Richmond's most used, every-slice-of-life urban park, and hundreds of fish of two distinct species — brown trout and rainbow trout — are being stocked together for the public's fish-catching enjoyment. Brown trout and rainbow trout: equally prized by the park's fishers.

So today it is with both apprehension and enthusiasm that I take my seat in Jasper's church. I find a space in a pew near the back. Seated to my right is a dark-suited man who greets me with a handshake and a grin and a "Welcome to Sixth Mount Zion." We exchange first names. His is Russell. I don't know it now, but this worship service will last 2 ½ hours during which I will not look at my watch. (Most of my former church experience has been in services that have lasted an hour.)

There are music and announcements and music and prayer and music and white-gowned dedications of two babies accompanied by 22 relatives. There is a multi-chorus children's choir performance of "Let's Go Higher and Higher in the Lord."

At one point in the service an energetic young girl strides to the front, takes the microphone, raises her eyebrows with an exuberant smile, and makes a three-word pronouncement of excitement: "It's offering time!"

Russell tells me that those of us who want to put an offering in the basket will file out of our pews in row-by-row procession and walk single-file down the aisle and deposit our gifts in the baskets that await there front and center as the pastor and the choir and the entire congregation all watch. I fold a bill and fall in line – as do most of the attendees.

Later is what I refer to as the Big Prayer – the altar call prayer. After announcements about concerns and requests, there is an invitation for anyone with special prayer needs to walk to the front and gather. I stay put. So does Russell. Perhaps 50 persons walk to the front. The lights dim and the congregation is told to hold hands. A well-dressed, 30-something couple has arrived late on my left and I hold hands with her on one side and with Russell on the other – for 15 minutes. At one point in the prayer something is said about "visitors in our congregation" and the woman's hand squeezes mine with welcoming acknowledgement.

The sermon arrives and Reverend Nelson — a handsome man just barely into his 30s — takes the pulpit with a humble and soft-spoken presence.

Have you ever seen the Grand Canyon? Then you know that no verbal or written or video description can do it justice. You simply have to be there. Same with Reverend Nelson's sermon.

I do expect an engaging style, an exciting presence, and compelling histrionics. And those are indeed firmly in place. But this sermon's foremost quality is its poignancy, its fresh and deeply thoughtful presentation of an essential truth, its philosophically intellectual depth, and its spiritual resonance. Plus, like a great symphony, its phrasing and movements vary with context, and carry the whole thing continually forward while building to a resonant climax that is sustained just the right amount.

This sermon rests on a Bible passage in the book of Daniel — one I've heard countless sermons about: the fiery furnace. Those three men whose poetic names have spawned a whole industry of derivatives — Shadrach, Meshach and Abednego — are cast into the furnace where, because of their belief and trust in God, they are unharmed.

I will later learn that Reverend John Jasper used this same text for a sermon he delivered at this church in July of 1884. I of course never heard Jasper preach, but those who did hear him attribute the same qualities to him that I now attribute to Reverend Nelson.

The sermon ends and so does the worship service and we respond to encouragement from the pulpit to hug our neighbors. Russell hugs me and so does the woman on my left.

My attendance at a service here was an important prerequisite to my publishing this new translation of "De Sun Do Move." In William Eldridge Hatcher's 1908 biography of Jasper, he said that thousands of persons from all over the nation visited Richmond every year, and they felt their visit wasn't complete without attending a worship service at Sixth Mount Zion Baptist Church.

Richmonder John Bryan has written for such publications as Sports Illustrated, Delta SKY, *and* Parade.Com. *His books include the 2007 Skyhorse publication,* Take Me Fishing, *that has an Introduction by Howell Raines and Foreword by Jimmy Carter. Longtime chief development officer for Virginia Commonwealth University's School of the Arts, and now president of the Arts Council of Richmond, Bryan has also served on the staffs of the American Sportfishing Association and, most recently, Baptist Theological Seminary at Richmond.*

Stephen Hawking's Position on All This *by John Bryan*

Stephen Hawking is the preeminent physicist of our time – the world's foremost theoretician on how the universe works. How would he respond to John Jasper's "De Sun Do Move"? We have some clues.

In his most recent book, his 2005 *A Briefer History of Time*, Hawking weighs in on what the Bible says about the sun moving and cites one of the passages on which Jasper rests his sermon. Hawking explains mankind's earliest attempts to explain the universe – including spirits inhabiting rivers and mountains and celestial bodies, and the need to gain their favor to ensure fertility and even sunshine. Hawking explains that eventually scientists discovered that precise physical laws order and govern these things, and, Hawking says, "The sun and the moon might still be gods, but they were gods who obeyed strict laws, apparently without any exceptions, if one discounts stories such as that of the sun stopping for Joshua."

Hawking explains that Galileo's public challenge of the church – specifically the notion that the earth is the center of the universe around which the sun and all else move – was the beginning of modern science. Galileo argued that the Bible's purpose has nothing to do with the delivery of scientific laws and theories – and in spite of the strong Church dictum to the contrary, the earth actually rotates around the sun, not the opposite. Of course the eventual development of powerful tools such as math and science and telescopes and computers confirmed not only the rotation of our solar system, but all sorts of other things that had long been mysteries. Hawking writes that God has always been "confined to the areas that … science [does] not understand."

Hawking further addresses the notion of God versus science – the question about God intervening in scientific laws, stopping and starting the sun for example: "If there were a complete set of [scientific] laws, that would infringe God's freedom to change His mind and intervene in the world. Yet, since God is all-powerful, couldn't God infringe on His freedom if He wanted to? It's a bit like the old paradox: can God make a stone so heavy He can't lift it?"

And Hawking addresses another disconnect: scientists versus theologians. "Does it [the universe] need a creator, and, if so, does He have any other effect on the universe? And who created Him? Up to now most scientists have been too occupied with the development of new theories that describe what the universe is to ask why. The people whose business it is to ask why … have not been able to keep up with the advance of scientific theories."

Using these types of passages, Hawking presents an almost subliminal theme: In spite of physicists' continuing and ever more accurate work on deciphering the laws that rule the universe, there will always be the recognition that a fundamental force must exist – "God" –

that caused it all to happen. And humans will never be able to understand the mystery of God.

And this is the precise point where Jasper and Hawking converge and agree: in spite of what the learned authorities say and "prove," there is still a God whose ultimate truth trumps all else.

I e-mailed Stephen Hawking and asked him to consider writing something for this booklet. I received the following response: "As you can imagine, Prof. Hawking receives many such [requests] every day. He very much regrets that due to the severe limitations he works under, and the enormous number of requests he receives, he is unable to compose a reply to every message, and we do not have the resources to deal with many of the specific scientific enquiries and theories we receive. Please see the website http://www.hawking.org.uk for more information about Professor Hawking, his life and his work. Yours faithfully, Sam Blackburn, Technical Assistant to Professor S.W. Hawking, Department of Applied Mathematics and Theoretical Physics, University of Cambridge, United Kingdom.

QUICK ORDER FORM

Please send _____ copies of *De Sun Do Move* to:

_____
Name

_____
Address

_____
City, State, Zip

_____
Telephone:

_____
E-mail:

Total Order:

      _____ copies $14.95 each $_____

      Shipping/handling @ $4 for the $_____
      the first book and $2 for each
      additional book

      TOTAL $_____

Enclose check or money order payable to ***Charles Creek Associates***.

Send to: **Charles Creek Associates**
                P.O. Box 25071
                Richmond, VA 23260-2571